A roof and

by Annette Smith
Photography by John Pettitt

This is **our** house.

The roof looks like this.

The windows are like this.

The door looks like this.

This is **my** house.

My house looks like this.

Here is the roof.

Here is a window,

and here is a door.

The path goes up to the door.

Come and see **our** garden.

The trees look like this 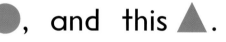, and this .

The fence goes around our garden, and here is the gate .

Come and see **my** house
and **my** garden.

Can **you** see a ■ and a ▮
and a ▲ and a ● ?